H. Turner.

FURTHER EVERYDAY PRAYERS

FURTHER EVERYDAY PRAYERS

Contributors
DAVID JENKINS
HENRY McKEATING
MICHAEL WALKER

Editor
HAZEL SNASHALL

INTERNATIONAL BIBLE READING ASSOCIATION
National Christian Education Council
Robert Denholm House
Nutfield, Redhill, Surrey, RH1 4HW

ACKNOWLEDGEMENTS

We are grateful for permission to include the following:

Verses from the *New English Bible* © 1970 (Oxford and Cambridge University Presses);
Verses from the *Good News Bible* © American Bible Society, New York, 1976 (The Bible Societies/Collins);
Verses from the *Revised Standard Version* © 1946 and 1952 Division of Christian Education, National Council of Churches of Christ in the USA;
Verses from *The Holy Bible, New International Version* © 1973, 1978 International Bible Society (Hodder and Stoughton);
Poem by Margaret Drake from *Beyond all Pain* by Cecily Saunders.

Unless otherwise indicated, biblical quotations are from the following versions:
The Nicene Creed — *Good News Bible*
Sharing the World with God — *New English Bible*
Occasional Prayers — *Revised Standard Version*

Cover photograph by Martin Snashall

Jenkins, David, *1941 Mar. 18—*
  Further everyday prayers.
  1. Prayer-books
  I. Title II. McKeating, Henry III. Walker, Michael, *1932—*
  IV. Snashall, Hazel
  242'.8   BV245

ISBN 0-7197-0495-2

ISBN 0-7197-0495-2
© 1987 National Christian Education Council

Typeset by Avonset, Midsomer Norton, Bath
Printed and bound by The Whitefriars Press Ltd, Tonbridge

CONTENTS

INTRODUCTION

'Lord, teach us to pray' (Luke 11.1, GNB). This was the request of the disciples when they had seen Jesus praying.

Most of us, like the disciples, need help to pray. We may find it difficult to discover and maintain a satisfactory pattern of prayer. Words sometimes do not come easily. When words do come, they often reflect what is uppermost in our minds and do not allow us to express and develop the fulness of our relationship with God.

In the end, the best way to learn to pray is to pray. We may only be able to renew our praying by praying. This book can help us. It gives a structure which can give a shape to our own praying. The words in the prayers are not substitutes for our own words. They are the starting point for meditation, reflection and words which are our own. In order for this to happen part of our practice of prayer must be to allow ourselves to be quiet in the presence of God.

The three contributors — David Jenkins, Henry McKeating and Michael Walker — offer their own experience of life, faith and prayer to help us to pray.

THE NICENE CREED

We believe . . .

'I assure you that if you have faith as big as a mustard seed, you can say to this hill, "Go from here to there!" and it will go. You could do anything.'   *(Matthew 17.20)*

Lord, we believe.
   But we confess we don't have the faith that moves mountains.
We believe.
   But sometimes you are not very real to us.
We believe.
   But sometimes all the other demands that keep crowding in on us make it hard to remember *your* demands.
We believe.
   But there are some things in the Christian faith that we don't find it easy to accept.

Lord, we believe — in our fashion.
Lord, we believe — help our unbelief.

When we say we believe, Lord, what we mean is that we want to live by whatever is your will for us, even though we aren't always sure what that will is.
When we say we believe, we mean we want to put you first; even if it doesn't always work out that way.
When we say we believe, we mean we want to be true to you. Keep us true to you — to *you,* not just to a set of statements about you.

Father, we pray for those who find faith more difficult than we do:
   for those who would like to believe; whose sympathies are with your people, but who find faith hard;
   for those who once believed, but have lost faith;
   for those who, in their heart of hearts, believe in you, but find the gospel too demanding to live by.

Father, we pray for all those who count themselves as believers. Help them to grow in faith, that they may become more truly yours.

Magnified and praised be the living God: he is, and there is no limit in time unto his being.

He is One, and there is no unity like unto his unity; inconceivable is he, and unending is his unity.

He hath neither bodily form nor substance: we can compare nought unto him in his holiness.

(The Authorised Daily Prayer Book: Jewish)

Lord, when we think about you, about what you really are, we are reduced to silence. We can only praise you, and adore.

We confess that most of the time we make no attempt to think about you at all; that we live our lives as though you did not exist.

We thank you that there is only one you, Lord, and that by your one will the world is governed. The universe keeps your laws, Lord. There are no other laws to keep but yours.

We confess that of all your creation, we, mankind, forget or disobey your laws, or try to make different ones of our own.

We can't imagine you, Lord. There is nothing in your world that we can really compare you with; no handle by which our minds can really get hold of you. There is no language that is really much use for speaking about you.

We can't imagine you, Lord — and yet you say you make us in your own image, and that everything you have made speaks of you.

We can't imagine you, Lord — yet we speak to you, and we believe you speak to us.

Lord, you are great enough for the needs of the universe. Hear our prayer for our tiny part of it: for our families, our friends, our neigbbours; for the people we work with, the ones we see in the shops or at the bus stop. We know some of the needs of some of these people. You know them all. Help us to show them your love, even if only by smiling at them.

> *The Lord is king.*
> > *He is clothed with majesty and strength.*
> *The earth is set firmly in place*
> > *and cannot be moved.*   *(Psalm 93.1)*
>
> *The Lord is my shepherd;*
> > *I have everything I need.*   *(Psalm 23.1)*

Lord of the world, you made everything, and you sustain it all.
I can depend on that.
You called your people out of slavery
and made them your own,
and have led and guided them ever since.
And you have led me too.
Looking back, I can see your hand in so many things.
Thanks be to you.

Lord of my life, you are with me now, in the present.
You are willing to lead me today, if I will let you.
Thanks be to you.

Lord of hope, for the future I have your promises,
and I know that you do not let people down,
and that you are able to do for me
far more that I can ask or think.
Thanks be to you.

You are my King, entitled to all my obedience.
You are my Father, worthy of all my love.

I pray today for people faced with difficult decisions; decisions which will seriously affect their lives and the lives of their loved ones: decisions about jobs, about their marriage, about where to live, about money.

I pray for those who can see no way through their problems; for whom it is all to much.

Help them to see that you, who control the universe, are in control of their lives, too.

Do you not know?
  Were you not told long ago?
  Have you not heard how the world began?
It was made by the one who sits on his throne
  above the earth and beyond the sky;
  the people below look as tiny as ants.
He stretched out the sky like a curtain,
  like a tent in which to live.   *(Isaiah 40.21-22)*

When we look at the universe, and at all the multitude of things that you have made, Lord, we confess to have much too great a sense of our own importance.

What does it feel like to be you, Lord?
  To scatter galaxies through space, like a child scattering the bubbles that he blows?
  To watch mountains rise and erode away again, as we watch sandcastles subside when the tide comes in?
  To number every microbe and virus; to be aware of every individual, whirling atom?
What does it feel like to be the choreographer of that great dance of creation?
  Lord, I can't imagine it. There is a great deal in the world, a very great deal, that I don't understand. It doesn't make sense to me. But you made it, and it all makes sense to you.

Father, I pray for all scientists and researchers
and seekers of knowledge,
who are trying to understand more about your universe.
Grant that the knowledge they gain
may make your world a better place
and not a worse one.

God's great goodness ay endureth,
  Deep his wisdom passing thought:
Splendour, light, and life attend him,
  Beauty springing out of nought.
    Evermore,
    From his store
  New-born worlds rise and adore.   *Joachim Neander*

Lord God, we praise you for those riches of your creation which we
shall never see:
  for stars whose light will never reach the earth;
  for species of living things that were born,
    and flourished, and perished,
    before mankind appeared in the world;
  for patterns and colours in the flowers,
    which only insect eyes are able to see;
  for strange, high music
    that human ears can never hear.
Lord God, you see everything that you have made, and behold it is
very good.

How many worlds might you have created, Lord,
of which we know nothing?
  How many suns and solar systems?
  How many earths teeming with life?
  How many civilisations, of beings beyond our comprehension?
  How many universes, with how many dimensions?
We thank you that here,
within the limitations of this universe,
this earth,
you have created beauty enough to satisfy our souls;
space enough in which do to your will,
and time enough in which to seek redemption.

Lord God, you have given us the visible world to use.
You have put it at our disposal.
Teach us to use your gifts wisely, and with respect,
and to share equitably what you have given us.

12

*God did what he had purposed, and made known to us the secret plan
he had already decided to complete by means of Christ. This plan,
which God will complete when the time is right, is to bring all
creation together, everything in heaven and on earth, with Christ as
head.*   *(Ephesians 1.9-10)*

Lord Jesus Christ, we address you as 'Lord' very glibly.
Teach us what your lordship really means.

Lord Jesus, you are one Lord, the same Lord, the Lord of us all, but
you mean so many different things to us. We can come to you, and
find all our needs fulfilled. We can turn to you at different times and
in different circumstances, and find you all in all.
    You have comfort where comfort is due,
        challenge where challenge is needed,
        strength for our weakness,
        healing for our disappointments,
        hope in our disillusionment.
Lord Jesus, Saviour of all and Judge of all, help us not just to fasten
on the aspects of you and of your message that we find most
congenial, but to face up to *all* you are and to all you have to say to
us; that we may worship not only one Christ, but the *whole* Christ, not
an image of Christ after our own hearts.

God our Father, we pray for those who have never appreciated the
riches which you offer them in your Son Jesus; those for whom he has
never become a reality:
    for those who have never been moved by the story of the cross, or
        felt the need of the forgiveness Jesus won for us;
    for those who leave the gospel aside as something that does not
        concern them; which they feel they can get on well enough
        without;
    for those for whom 'Christ' is only a swear-word.
For all these, and for all who do not pray for themselves, accept our
intercessions, through Jesus Christ our Lord.

'Believe me when I say that I am in the Father and the Father is in me.
If not, believe because of the things I do.'   *(John 14.11)*

Lord Jesus Christ, Son of the Father, we thank you for your perfect obedience to your Father's will, by which you won for us salvation. Lord, we cannot even imagine what perfect obedience really means; much less can we imitate you. Forgive what we are, and may our inadequacy be lost in your perfection.

Human experience isn't really the same, can't be the same, as yours, Lord. Yet you did make us in your own image, and you have taught us that what we are like can give us clues as to what you are like.
When we have a child, what do we feel for him? We welcome him as ours; he is part of us, our flesh and blood, and will be so, to his life's end, and ours.
What do we hope for him? We hope that he will grow, and learn, mature, and be himself. We hope, and trust, that he will be true to himself, but being true to himself, will also be true to us, who have given him life.
We hope and trust that, as we love him he will love us, and love what we love, respect what we respect; care about what we care about.
Because he is ours, part of us, our flesh and blood, to our life's end his joys will be our joys. We shall take pride in all his achievements. His pain will be our pain; his loss our loss. In all his affliction we shall be afflicted.
Are we on the right track, Lord? Are these the clues we should be looking for?

Your Son is one with you; closer to you than any human child to human parent. True to himself; true to you; his delight always to do your will; loving what you love; his work your work. His willingness to pay the cost is your willingness; his pain your pain; his accomplishment your accomplishment.

Thanks be to God for his inexpressible gift!

For the divine nature was his from the first.

(Philippians 2.6, NEB)

We thank you, Lord, Father, Son and Holy Spirit, that you were there
from the beginning; that before the world was ever made, you bore
the name and nature of its Saviour.

Father, sometimes we are inclined to write people off,
and there are situations of which we despair.
There are people who seem so totally prejudiced
that it is useless even trying to understand
their point of view,
let alone getting them to change their minds.
There are some who appear so hopelessly misguided
that there is no point in attempting
to educate them or persuade them.
There are situations which are so bad,
and which have been bad for so long,
that we feel it futile to try to get to the bottom of them,
to say nothing of endeavouring to put them right.

Maker and Saviour, we thank you that you do not write off your
creation, or anything in it, and that you do not despair of the world
you have made.
Lord Jesus Christ, if from the beginning you were there, nothing in
the created world can be irredeemable.
We pray for all those people who, whether they think of themselves
in that way or not, are helping with your redeeming work:
for conciliators, trying to increase understanding;
for negotiators, attempting to produce settlements acceptable to
all;
for those working to reduce tension in the world.
We pray for those struggling to right wrongs, especially other
people's wrongs:
for MPs and councillors who take up the cases of aggrieved
constituents;
for reformers who have a vision of how things might be done
better, and who work to that end.
May none of them grow weary.

15

. . . God from God, Light from Light, true God from true God, begotten not made, of one Being with the Father. Day 9

Christ is the visible likeness of the invisible God. He is the first-born Son, superior to all created things. *(Colossians 1.15)*

Father, you are invisible;
    but we thank you that we can see you in Christ.
You are beyond our reach;
    but we thank you that in Christ we are in touch with you.
You are beyond our thoughts;
    but we thank you that in Christ we can grasp something of what
    you are.

Jesus, you have a hundred titles,
    all of them meaningful,
    all of them with something to say to us.
We call you Master, and Lord,
    Saviour, Redeemer and Teacher,
    Messiah, Servant of God,
    our great High Priest, Prophet and King,
    Friend of sinners,
    Lamb of God.
You are all these, and more, more than we have words for. You are
God's very Son, sharing his being and essence; his true nature. You
are God himself: truly God.

Lord, stretch our minds.
Make us think, Lord.
Prick us to look again at the phrases that trip off our tongues in church
    and see them with fresh eyes.
Make us alive to the huge things we say and sing.
When we are letting familiar words wash over us, wake us up to the
    enormity of what they are telling us.
Lord, what you are and what you have done are more than our little
    brains can properly get hold of. But stimulate us at least to make
    the effort.

For through him God created everything in heaven and on earth, the seen and the unseen things, including spiritual powers, lords, rulers, and authorities. God created the whole universe through him and for him. Christ existed before all things, and in union with him all things have their proper place. *(Colossians 1.16-17)*

Lord, you have taught us that everything we ask of you should be 'through Jesus Christ our Lord':
    that everything we do we must do *in his name*.
Only so are our prayers the kind of prayers you are pleased to grant:
    only so are our actions the actions you approve.

We thank you, Father, that you have given us an example;
that everything you created was created through your Son;
that everything you do is done in his name.
Thus we know that whatever you have done,
    or are doing, or will do,
from the first moment of creation to the end of time,
love is the point of it all.

Lord and Father,
    through Christ you created us,
    and put love in our very natures.
    Show us how better to express that love in prayer.
    Help us to examine our prayers,
    that the desires of our love may be tested by your love,
    so that our love asks only what your love wills.

    Make love the point of all our lives.

For us men and for our salvation he came down from heaven . . .
Day 11

You know the grace of our Lord Jesus Christ; rich as he was, he made himself poor for your sake, in order to make you rich by means of his poverty. *(2 Corinthians 8.9)*

I feel very sorry for them, the poor of the earth;
   for the people who live in shacks, in shanty towns, without bathrooms, without proper toilets, without running water.
I feel sorry for the peasants of the third world, working hard to farm a few acres for an income of a few pounds a month.
I feel sorry for the people who have to walk miles to fetch every drop of water they use: water in all probability full of germs and parasites.
I feel sorry, desperately sorry, for people whose country is hit by drought and famine, and who have to watch their children die, without being able to do anything about it.

I feel sorry for them all.
   But could I go and live with them?
   Live like them?
   Be one of them?
   Could I make their insecurity my insecurity?
   Their hunger my hunger?
   Their expectations my expectations?
I feel sorry for them, but could I, if it would do them any good, give up my lifestyle: my pleasant home with all its comforts; my income; my eating habits; my television and my hi-fi?
   Could I give up the reassuring knowledge of a health service to rely on when I am ill?

What sort of love would it need to do a thing like that?
More love than I've got.

   Unsearchable the love
      That hath the Saviour brought;
   His grace is far above
      Or man or angels' thought:
   Suffice for us that God, we know,
   Our God, is manifest below.   *(Charles Wesley)*

The angel answered, 'The Holy Spirit will come on you, and God's power will rest upon you. For this reason the holy child will be called the Son of God.'   *(Luke 1.35)*

Lord, Holy Spirit, we thank you that wherever men or women respond with obedience and faith, you are there. That whenever we open ourselves to you in expecation, you are present with us.

> You responded to the faith of Mary, making her the mother of our Lord.
>
> You responded to the obedience of Jesus in fulfilling all righteousness and being baptised. You came upon him like a dove.
>
> You responded to the faith and expectancy of the apostles, coming upon them at Pentecost, filling them with your strength and sending them into all the world.

Give us the same humility and obedience, that through us you may accomplish the things that you want done.

Lord, Holy Spirit, when God spoke the world into being,
> you were there, moving on the face of the waters.

When God spoke through the prophets,
> it was you who inspired them.

When at last he spoke to us through his Son,
> you were there, for by your power he became incarnate.

When the gospel was preached by the apostles to all nations,
> it was at your direction.

Lord of all communication, give grace to all who communicate truth. Inspire your preachers, so that they offer the gospel in words of urgency and power. Give skill and clarity to those who teach. And to those who have little to say, but display the gospel by their Christian lives, give cheerful constancy.

*God purposely chose what the world considers nonsense in order to
shame the wise, and he chose what the world considers weak in order
to shame the powerful. He chose what the world looks down on and
despises, and thinks is nothing, in order to destroy what the world
thinks is important.   (1 Corinthians 1.27-28)*

*He has stretched out his mighty arm
    and scattered the proud with all their plans.
He has brought down mighty kings from their thrones,
    and lifted up the lowly.
He has filled the hungry with good things,
    and sent the rich away with empty hands.   (Luke 1.51-53)*

Lord, you do not do things our way,
        or judge by our standards,
        or display our sense of priorities.
Help us to see things your way,
        to judge (if we judge at all) by your standards;
        to make your priorities our priorities.
Make us not too timid to look at the world through your eyes and see
it upside down; that we may not lay waste our powers getting and
spending but, by giving and being spent, may grow and become
strong.

We pray, Lord, for the society to which we belong, that we may be
        enabled to reshape it after your own heart.
    Show us how we can give the most to those whose needs are
        greatest;
    how we can best relieve those who bear the heaviest burdens;
    and how we can most justly share the rich resources you have put
        at our disposal.

'I am the Lord's servant,' said Mary; 'may it happen to me as you have said.'
(Luke 1.38)

All she said was, 'Yes':
    'Yes' to what you asked of her,
    'Yes' to the plans you had for her,
    'Yes' to what little she knew of your will for the world.

Response of perfect faith!

Her 'Yes' brought to fruition plans made before the universe was created.
Her 'Yes' answered your mercy's whole design.
Her 'Yes' brought forth the first-born of all creation.

And all the promises of God find their 'Yes' in him.

For the right faith is, that we believe and confess: that our Lord Jesus Christ, the Son of God, is God and Man; God, of the substance of the Father, begotten before the worlds: and Man, of the substance of his mother, born in the world.   *(Quicunque Vult)*

We praise you, Lord Jesus Christ, because you were, like us, of human flesh; that you knew, like us, hunger and thirst, pain and distress.

Like us you knew loneliness,

the need of friends and of companionship;

you were familiar with all human needs and desires.

We praise you that unlike us you were not controlled by these things. Your food and drink was to do the will of him who sent you. All human wants were second to doing what the Father wanted you to do.

You were tempted in every way that we are.

Unlike us you remained without sin.

Lord, you became Man, like us; unlike us, *perfect* Man.

Lord Jesus Christ, you became Man, like us, in order to show us what we were meant to be. Make us so grow in grace that we become truly what you are.

> Dear Master, in whose life I see
> All that I would, but fail to be,
> Let thy clear light for ever shine,
> To shame and guide this life of mine.
>
> Though what I dream and what I do
> In my weak days are always two,
> Help me, oppressed by things undone,
> O thou, whose deeds and dreams were one.
>
> *John Hunter*

'Worthy is the Lamb who was slain, to receive power and wealth and wisdom and might and honour and glory and blessing!'

(Revelation 5.12)

Lord, we know all about the suffering in the world. We are not allowed to forget it: the newspapers, radio, and especially television, thrust it at us every day.

Suffering is news. Much of the news is suffering.

Accidents, disasters, crimes, terrorism: all of them news.

All of them suffering — for somebody.

Then there are the political protests, all of them protests against
suffering of one sort or another:

against denial of human rights; against oppression;

against unjust laws; against imprisonment without trial;

against exploitation or discrimination.

We are left in no doubt about it, Lord, the suffering of the world, your world. So much of it seems to be placarded before us.

But you know it all:

not only the suffering that is news,

but the suffering that is not news;

the loss that is not worth a headline;

the unspectacular bereavement;

the ordinary death;

the injustices unreported;

the poverty and distress that are taken for granted,

because they are always there.

Lord, you know it all, and you feel for all, for all your children.

Lord Jesus Christ, you not only know *about* suffering, you *know* suffering.

You know the power of the autocratic State.

You know the rigged trial,

the unjust sentence,

and death by torture.

Praise be to you that on your Father's throne you bear your scars, and take that tortured manhood into God.

It was towards evening when Joseph of Arimathea arrived. He . . .
bought a linen sheet, took the body down, wrapped it in the sheet, and
placed it in a tomb which had been dug out of solid rock. Then he
rolled a large stone across the entrance to the tomb.

(Mark 15.42,46)

We thank you, Lord Jesus Christ, Son of God, that you shared every
experience of humankind.
We praise you for the courage of others who, like you, accept death,
or risk death, for good reasons and worthwhile ends.

You weren't pretending, Lord. You weren't, like some indestructible
superman, just going through the motions, knowing it would be all
right in the end.
It was real.
You were destroyed; torn apart on a cross; dead; buried. The last rites
were performed, rather hurriedly, it is true. Your mother had no
doubts, nor your friends. They knew it was the end of you.

And you?
You died in faith, as I shall do; not knowing, only trusting.

Father, it is your will that we should all die.
We thank you for those who die after a good life,
    old and full of years.
We pray for those who die young and with promise unfulfilled;
    for victims of tragedy and disaster.
We pray for those who die burdened by regrets or by resentment.
Give strength to those for whom death is a slow agony.
Give peace to those who die suddenly, and without warning.
Comfort those who must watch others die, and cannot help them.

Lord Jesus Christ, you have been through everything.
Stay with me through everything.

On the third day he rose again in accordance with the Scriptures . . .

When thou tookest upon thee to deliver man, thou didst not abhor the virgin's womb.
(Te Deum)

She wrapped him in swaddling clothes, and laid him in a manger.
(Luke 2.7)

When they came to the place called 'The Skull', they crucified Jesus there.
(Luke 23.33)

They took the body of Jesus, and bound it in linen cloths.
(John 19.40, RSV)

And stooping to look in, he saw the linen cloths lying there.
(John 20.5, RSV)

Lord, you are free:
   free of the confining tomb,
     the tight swaddling clothes,
     the narrow cradle;
   loosed from the transfixing cross;
   free now of grave cloths,
     and the close tomb.
You are no longer bound even to one place, one time.
You are let loose in all the world.
You have overflowed our universe;
   and behold,
   the heaven and the heaven of heavens
   cannot contain you.

Lord, make us free:
   free to share your new life,
   free to be the people you meant us to be;
   that, being risen with you,
     we may seek the things that are above.

Elijah said to Elisha, 'Tell me what you want me to do for you before I am taken away.'

'Let me receive the share of your power that will make me your successor,' Elisha answered.

'That is a difficult request to grant,' Elijah replied. 'But you will receive it if you see me as I am being taken away from you.'

(2 Kings 2.9-10)

After saying this, he (Jesus) was taken up to heaven as they watched him. *(Acts 1.9)*

Whoever believes in me will do what I do — yes, he will do even greater things, because I am going to the Father. *(John 14.12)*

We thank you, Lord, for your witnesses, the apostles. They were there; we were not; and we depend on their testimony. If they had not preached your word with power, we could never have received it. We thank you for their faith, for without theirs, ours would not be possible.

Lord, great are your promises:
they comfort us, they sustain us.
But some of them are astonishing;
so astonishing that we dare not grasp them.
Some of your promises do not comfort,
but challenge our complacency.
  Ought we to be doing greater works than yours?
  Can we?
  You have said so.

Lord Jesus, you have returned to your Father and our Father, but you have left us your power. We confess that we cannot bring ourselves to hold out our hands to receive it. We know a little, but all too little, of what you offer us. Give us the willingness to receive, that we may know what are the greater things you want us to do, and in your strength may do them.

And so, in honour of the name of Jesus
  all beings in heaven, on earth, and in the world below
  will fall on their knees,
and all will openly proclaim that Jesus Christ is Lord,
  to the glory of God the Father.   *(Philippians 2.10-11)*

Look, he is coming on the clouds! Everyone will see him.
                                                (Revelation 1.7)

God our Father,
we thank you that though we do not yet
see all things subject to you,
we do see Jesus,
and can already belong to his kingdom,
respect his authority,
live by his laws.

We confess that we do not always behave as citizens of the kingdom.
Too much of our time we live our lives according to the standards of
this world, and the desires of the world govern our lives. Help us to
see that here we have no abiding city, but that our loyalty is to a better
and a heavenly order.

   Make us true to what we really know, and to the kingdom that in
our better moments we genuinely serve.

Lord Jesus Christ, even now you sit on your Father's throne.
You are sovereign —
but only we who believe acknowledge your rule.

May your kingdom come.
May your will be done on earth as it is in heaven.
Hasten the time when every eye shall see you,
                        every knee shall bow, and
                        every tongue acknowledge your sovereignty.

Judge therefore yourselves, brethren, that ye be not judged of the Lord. *(The Book of Common Prayer)*

We thank you, Lord, that you have made us accountable for all we do. We thank you that you have given us ample guidance about how we should live.

You have given us your law, and the example of your saints.

You have given us the teaching and example of our Lord and Saviour.

Therefore we are without excuse.

We confess to you that sometimes we create problems for ourselves. We persuade ourselves that to know what is right and what is wrong is very difficult. Remind us, Lord, that most of the time we have no problems in knowing how we *ought* to behave.

Lord, when there are really difficult issues to decide,

concentrate our minds,

stimulate our prayers,

make us open to each other's opinions and insights;

and give us the guidance of your Holy Spirit.

But take away our excuses.

When we are manufacturing the problems, call our bluff.

Lord, do not allow us to comfort ourselves with the thought that the day of judgement is a long way off. Teach us to live every moment as though in your presence, and to take every decision as though we must answer immediately to you.

But remind us, Father, that the judgement is the judgement of your Son, Jesus Christ, who gave himself for us; and that the wrath which we must fear is the wrath of the Lamb.

Father, we pray for those people who seem to have no conscience; those who commit hideous crimes. We pray for those who in less serious ways seem to have little regard for right and wrong. Enlighten their minds and hearts, as only you can.

We pray for those whose consciences are overburdened, who condemn themselves, though you do not condemn. Give them your divine sense of proportion.

. . . and his kingdom will have no end.

Christ rules . . . above all heavenly rulers, authorities, powers and lords; he has a title superior to all titles of authority in this world and in the next.
(Ephesians 1.21)

Praise be to you, Son of God, Son of Man,
because to you is given dominion and glory and kingdom.
Your dominion is an everlasting dominion
which shall not pass away,
and your kingdom one that shall not be destroyed.

Lord, when we look round at the world in which we live, we cannot help being anxious and troubled about many things. We see so much that cries out to be put right; so many oppressive powers that need to be overthrown.

We know all this is true; and we know that it is our Christian job to be on the side of the oppressed, and to be hungry to see right prevail. But give us, too, your sense of perspective, to see that the powers that dominate the world, even the most potent of them, are very transitory. They will perish, but you endure; they will all wear out like a garment. You change them like old clothes, and they pass away. But you are the same, and your years have no end.

Father, we pray for the oppressed; for those who have been treated harshly by other people or by circumstances; for those who have no freedom; who were born in a poverty from which they cannot escape; for those who have never had a chance.

We pray for those who cannot wait; who have waited too long, for justice, for liberty; for those who feel that only by violence can they hope to gain what is theirs by right. In their impatience give them wisdom, and in their just struggle give them the charity not to deny justice to others.

We pray for those who meet oppression with resignation; who assume that nothing can be done. Lord, give them hope, and give them self-respect, and give the knowledge that with you there is salvation.

> *Thou from the first*
> *Wast present, and, with mighty wings outspread,*
> *Dove-like sat'st brooding on the vast Abyss,*
> *And mad'st it pregnant.*
>
> *(John Milton, 'Paradise Lost')*

Lord, Holy Spirit, we praise you.

All life is your life, for all life comes from you.

All beauty is your beauty; for there is no beauty without you. The beauty of the natural world; the beauty that men think they create, in art, in literature, in music, and in anything else that they do — all comes from you and is prompted by you.

All good inspiration comes from you; all worthy impulses. Whether men believe it or not, give you credit or not, everything of value they achieve, you inspire.

All good thoughts are yours. Whatever of good mankind has accomplished or even contemplated, is of you.

Lord, as by your special grace going before us you have put good desires into our minds, so by your grace may we bring them to fruition.

Lord, we pray for all who try to create beauty in the world;

for all who organise, trying to produce order instead of disorder;

for all who try to bring wisdom and enlightenment;

for educators and all seekers of truth;

for all who nurture life, in the bringing up of children or in the healing of the sick.

Lord, Holy Spirit, all these are your people and do your work in the world.

*The spirit of the Lord took control of Gideon, and he blew a
trumpet . . .*
                                              (Judges 6.34)

God, give us your energy.
Giver of life, pity our lifelessness.

We thank you for your people who in times past were taken over by
your Spirit, and accomplished great things which they had not
dreamed of:
    who through your Spirit conquered kingdoms, stopped the mouths
        of lions, quenched raging fire, escaped the edge of the sword.
We thank you for those who by your Spirit's power suffered great
things:
    who through your Spirit suffered mocking and scourging, chains
        and imprisonment, and went about destitute, afflicted, ill-treated.
Lord, so fill us with your Spirit that we may not be altogether
unworthy of those who have gone before us.

Lord, forgive us that so much of our activity is just rushing around,
trying to keep up with the hundred and one things we feel need to be
done. Teach us the difference between your energy and our frantic
busy-ness. Show us what it is that you are calling us to do, so that we
may do it, not with all our might, but with all your might.

We commend to your care all those who find life too much for them;
    those who daily have to face jobs with which they cannot cope;
    those who are daunted by the whole business of living;
    those whose families make demands on them which they cannot
        meet;
    those who cannot summon up the strength to do the things they
        know have to be done;
    those who feel they cannot go on.
Lord, giver of life, give them life.

'The Helper will come — the Spirit, who reveals the truth about God and who comes from the Father. I will send him to you from the Father, and he will speak about me.' (John 15.26)

We thank you, Lord Holy Spirit, for all your work in us.
You have faced us with God's holy law,
and with the demand of the Father
that we should be perfect in his sight.
You have convinced us of our sin,
and of our need for grace.
You have convinced us, too, that grace is there,
offered to us through the Son,
sufficient for all our needs.

We confess that your challenge needs to be renewed daily;
daily we have fresh need of repentance;
daily we have new sins to be forgiven;
daily we have fresh need of the Son's justifying grace.
We are too hesitant, still, to trust your love.

May your refining fire, Spirit of God,
work through our lives and characters,
purifying everything.
May we through you continue to grow in grace.
Lead us on still towards holiness.

With the Father and the Son he is worshipped and glorified.

*'Go, then, to all peoples everywhere and make them my disciples:
baptise them in the name of the Father, the Son, and the Holy Spirit.'*
(Matthew 28.19)

Lord, we thank you that you did not reserve your salvation for your
ancient people the Jews. Being rich in mercy, you have shown the
immeasurable riches of your grace to us also. We who once were far
off have been brought near in the blood of Christ. Through him we
too have access in one Spirit to the Father.

Lord, from the beginning
you thrust your people out into the world.
In your strength they journeyed everywhere.
In your strength they faced constant dangers;
   of beatings and imprisonment,
   toil and hardship,
   cold and exposure,
   sleeplessness and hunger.
You gave them no rest.
But they had you to rely on.
Give to us, their successors,
the same urgency to speak your word,
the same eagerness to share what we know.

Be present with all whose special job it is to preach your gospel,
in this country or in others.
Be present with all Christians,
so that they cannot help spreading your word wherever they may be,
whether at work, at leisure,
or in friendly conversation,
so that their light may shine before men
and by it you may be glorified.
May the day quickly come when all your promises are fulfilled,
and you are worshipped and glorified in all the world, Father, Son
and Holy Spirit.

When . . . the Spirit comes, who reveals the truth about God, he will lead you into all the truth.   *(John 16.14)*

They were all filled with the Holy Spirit and began to talk in other languages, as the Spirit enabled them to speak.   *(Acts 2.4)*

Lord and Spirit, we thank you for the witness of your prophets, who through your inspiration looked forward to events more wonderful than even they could properly grasp.

We thank you for the witness of all those who have been able to trace your hand in events, and see your purposes being worked out in the world.

We thank you for the way you have led us, ourselves, and helped us to see the truth of scripture, and brought us to faith in Christ.

We pray that,
as you have made known the truth to us,
through others,
so you might make known the truth to others,
through us;
that you would give us your power to communicate,
to make clear to others the faith by which we live.

We pray for those through whom the scriptures are mediated to us today:
> for translators, that they may faithfully represent the word of God,
> for scholars who study and preachers who expound,
>> that they may enable the scriptures to speak powerfully to our time and to our condition.

We pray for every reader of the Bible, that each may search diligently and humbly, and continue to find spiritual food.

By speaking the truth in a spirit of love, we must grow up in every way to Christ, who is the head. Under his control all the different parts of the body fit together, and the whole body is held together by every joint with which it is provided. So when each separate part works as it should, the whole body grows and builds itself up through love.
(Ephesians 4.15-16)

Father, we thank you for your Church; for that company of faithful people who have, through the centuries, followed the way of life set out for them in your Son.

We confess that we, your people, are not what we ought to be.
    You have declared us 'one',
        but though we all acknowledge Jesus as Lord,
        in many ways we are divided.
    You have called us 'holy',
        but we are not yet holy in all we do,
        or obedient in all we undertake.
    We call ourselves 'catholic',
        but too often we are more attached to our own ways,
        and prouder of our own peculiarities,
        than to confessing the faith of the universal Church.
    We claim to be 'apostolic',
        but do not always show the single-minded faith
        of those in whose footsteps we profess to follow.
Lord, forgive all these our shortcomings, and our lack of zeal for your gospel.

We pray for all who sincerely call themselves Christian,
in whatever country, and of whatever race;
whatever their peculiarites of worship or of organisation.
Help us all to see what is important in your eyes,
and what is trivial.
Bring us all closer to you,
and so closer to each other.

*By our baptism, then, we were buried with him and share his death,
in order that, just as Christ was raised from death by the glorious
power of the Father, so also we might live a new life.*

(Romans 6.4)

Father, I thank you that I am yours —
that you have *made* me yours.

You have taught me something of your truth.
You have led me in your way.
You have poured out on me your grace.

You have offered me more of your truth
than I have yet had faith to grasp.
You have led me where I have not always been brave enough
or trusting enough to follow.
Your love has poured out on me more riches
than I have yet found love to respond to.

Lord, there are promises between us, not yet wholly fulfilled:
   my promises to you,
      of commitment and fidelity;
   your promises to me,
      which I am not open enough
      to let you keep to the full.

Lord, I *am* yours.
Lord, *make* me yours.

Naaman's servants went up to him and said, 'Sir, if the prophet had told you to do something difficult, you would have done it. Now why can't you just wash yourself, as he said, and be cured?'

(2 Kings 5.13)

Lord, make me whole.
I am not whole.
I am not the person you meant me to be.
I am incomplete, not grown to the maturity you planned for me.
You planted in me capacities I have not developed,
abilities which I have never exploited.
My senses are not as sharp as you designed them to be.
I do not perceive the richnesses of your creation,
the splendour you have bestowed on all you have made.
I am not as sensitive to wrong as I might be.
I am not perceptive of the needs and feelings
of those around me.
I do not hear, I do not dare to hear,
all the things you say to me, the calls that come to me.
I dare not hear,
in case you make demands I feel unable to meet.
I am weaker than you meant me to be,
because I have never accepted the strength you offered.

Lord, forgive what I am,
forgive me for what I have not become.
You have made it so easy, to wash and be clean.
Why do I make it so hard for myself,
to be immersed in the tide of your love?

We look for the resurrection of the dead, and the life of the world to come.

We are now God's children, but it is not yet clear what we shall become. But we know that when Christ appears, we shall be like him, because we shall see him as he really is. *(1 John 3.2)*

All of us, then, reflect the glory of the Lord with uncovered faces; and that same glory, coming from the Lord, who is the Spirit, transforms us into his likeness in an ever greater degree of glory.
(2 Corinthians 3.18)

It is a climb, Lord, this Christian pilgrimage.
    Sometimes a hard climb,
    sometimes an exhilarating climb,
but a climb, nearly all of the way.
Sometimes we can barely see the next step ahead.
Let us not be afraid, Lord, when we enter the cloud.
If we have to concentrate most of the time
just on keeping our footing,
don't let us forget where we are going.
A climb must lead to a summit,
and at the summit we shall see you as you really are.
Lord, it will be good for us to be there, and with unveiled faces to behold your glory, and to be transfigured into your likeness.

SHARING THE WORLD WITH GOD

THE PLACE WHERE WE LIVE

For parents of young children   **Day 1**

*Then he went back with them to Nazareth, and continued to be under
their authority; his mother treasured up all these things in her heart.
As Jesus grew up he advanced in wisdom and in favour with God and
man.* *(Luke 2.51-52)*

A thanksgiving
Father, in the life we have received from you, you have given us the
power to create new life, a seed sown in love that becomes a child
who is part of us.

For the awesome joy of that gift,
    thank you, Father.
For the energetic, inquisitive, mirthful, messy,
unpredictable delights of childhood,
    thank you, Father.
For those who find joy in their children and are
faithful in their parenthood,
    thank you, Father.

A parental prayer
Lord, the life we hold in our arms is the life you have given to us in
trust. This child is not our property to use for the fulfilment of our
own ambitions; this child is yours, whom one day you will call to
confess your name and become your disciple. May we be wise in
these short years when our influence will be more important than
anyone else's. In our love may our child begin to learn the perfect
love that casts out fear. In the life that we share as a family, in our
talking together, our eating together, our journeying together, and in
the disciplines we impose, may our child learn that we are worthy of
trust.

Intercession
Remember one-parent families, families under emotional or financial
stress, families where children are brutally maltreated, families that
are divided, families with children who are mentally or physically
handicapped.

39

Help us to seek what Jesus sought,
Things holy and of lasting worth,
The love that brings good will to men,
The deeds that make for peace on earth.

J. Waugh Boden

A thanksgiving
Father, we bless you for the priceless gift of education passed on from one generation to another.

For words and speech through which we can see into one
another's thought and experience,
thank you.
For the knowledge that teaches us how the world is made
and how we belong to it,
thank you.
For the skills by which we harness and direct the world's
energies and resources,
thank you.

May our children learn how to use words with imagination, truth and accuracy.

May they see the ways in which knowledge can benefit human beings and understand, too, how its abuse can destroy them.

May they gain those skills that, in their own generation, will make the world happier, safer and more just.

A teacher's prayer
Lord, as I teach others may I remember the ways through which I learned. May I feel the excitement of my pupils as they encounter new ideas and may I understand their difficulties in grasping those things they find obscure. Remind me of my responsibilities. May I not try to force children into my way of thinking but help them to learn how to think for themselves. May I create a learning environment, sufficiently open for children not to feel intimidated, sufficiently disciplined for every child to have the freedom to learn.

Intercession
Pray for the schools near to you, for their teaching staffs, governing bodies, and children.

'Remember — you were young once.'

A confession

Lord, I quickly forget the way it was when I was young. If I could remember, I might be more patient, more perceptive. As it is, I see only 'problems' —

     loud music, bizarre hair-styles,
     rebellious behaviour, violence,
     different moral values.

Forgive me, when that is all I see and when I am blind to or ignore everything else —

     idealism,
     enthusiasm,
     commitment,
     hard work.

Forgive me, Lord, when I am the 'problem'.

Intercession

Father, we pray for young people growing up in a difficult and dangerous world.

We pray for those who are unemployed, who have not worked since they left school and have never earned their own money.

We pray for those who are taking their first steps in their skill, trade or profession.

We pray for those who feel they have no support from the adults around them and who grow resentful at what they see to be their indifference.

We pray for those who are caught up in violence either giving it or receiving it.

We pray for those who are morally confused and uncertain of what is right or wrong.

We pray for young Christians as they strive to live out their faith in an unsympathetic world.

Father, you are head of all the family. Hear our prayers in Jesus' name.

For ourselves

Lord, may age not make us invulnerable and certain only of our own rightness.

That evening after sunset they brought to him all who were ill . . . and the whole town was there, gathered at the door. He healed many who suffered from various diseases. *(Mark 1.32-34)*

A thanksgiving

Lord, we thank you for the great resources of healing that are available to those who are sick.

For the skill of surgeons and the technical abilities of support staff in operating theatres,
> thank you.

For medical knowledge and the healing power of drugs and medicines, for chemists and pharmacists,
> thank you.

For nursing staff, for their professional skill and their capacity for caring and encouraging,
> thank you.

For support teams of physiotherapists, occupational therapists, radiologists, hospital social workers and hospital chaplains,
> thank you.

For admininstrative staff, ward orderlies, hospital porters and ambulance drivers,
> thank you.

A reflection

Lord, be with me when disease affects my body or my mind and they become strangers to me. May I have the strength to reassure those who love me and for whom my illness is a cause of deep anxiety. May I have the courtesy to co-operate with those who are responsible for my healing and behave in no way to make their task more dificult. At the same time, may I acknowledge a continuing responsibility for my own body and mind, and not be fearful of its secrets or hand over its welfare unquestioningly to others. Above all, may I trust in your healing presence, knowing that you work through all that is being done for me.

Quite suddenly, off the cuff, it came to me,
'Midst our laughing, chattering, joking and repartee,
The cheery 'See yer!' 'Take care!' and 'Good-byee!'
A sudden silence, slow unwinding, blessed peace and solitude.
(*Written by Margaret Drake, a few days before she died in St Christopher's Hospice, South London.*)

A thanksgiving
Father, accept our thanks for the hospice movement and its ministry to those who are terminally ill.
We thank you for all medical and auxiliary staff, for the skill with which they do their work, for the environment of hope with which they surround their patients and for the inner experience of peace they communicate even to the most fearful.
We thank you for all engaged in research into pain control, whose discoveries lift cruel burdens from those who suffer and guard the dignity of those who are close to death.
We thank you for all spiritual counsellors, for ministers and priests, for particularly gifted lay people and for members of religious orders especially committed to the care of the dying.

Intercession
Lord, may those who are dying know that you are very close.
Be with those whose minds are clear and whose senses are still alert. May the presence of those they love and the beauty and joy of the world glimpsed through the windows, all be signs of that love and glory that await us in paradise.
Be with those who journey through a twilight world, seemingly beyond everything save our touch and the words we whisper in their ear. May our touch be to them the strong grasp of Christ and our words an echo of his truth, now beyond all words.
Be present in the hour of death and grant a serene journey to all travellers to your eternal kingdom. Be with those who remain, for their grief is hard to bear.

'I now see how true it is that God has no favourites, but that in every nation the man who is godfearing and does what is right is acceptable to him.'   *(Acts 10.34-35)*

A thanksgiving
Father of all nations, who created us in all our diversity, who marked out the limits of our lands and seas, who hears our prayers, offered in our different languages, accept our thanks for one another:
> for the opportunity given us in the modern world
>> to understand one another
>> and to grow together as never before;
> for the privilege of bearing one another's burdens
>> and understanding one another's needs;
> for all who build bridges between people
>> of different races, culture and religion.

A reflection
Lord, teach me to face my own prejudices and to overcome them. Because Christ has made us his brothers and sisters, may I be a peacemaker and so be numbered amongst those who are called your children.

Intercession
Lord, bless all ethnic minorities within our own society.
> We pray for their community and religious leaders that they may faithfully represent their people.
> We pray for people of other religions that they may always have the freedom to worship according to their beliefs and customs.
> We pray for young people, especially when they are torn between the culture of their families and the culture within which they are growing up.
> We pray for inner city communities, especially where there is poverty, high unemployment and tension.

Lord, may we enrich one another, care for one another, and protect one another, in the name of Christ our Lord.

A thanksgiving

Father, we thank you that, out of the seas and from the earth, we receive the provision you have made for all our needs.

> We thank you for the skills in harvesting the earth's resources that people have passed on from one generation to another.
>
> We thank you for those through whose vision and work the products of our harvesting are channelled into areas of need.

Intercession

Lord, we pray for all communities that farm the land.

Bless farmers and farm-workers as they work their land and care for their livestock. Guide them in the decisions they make about their farming methods, their policy on fertilisers and insecticides, and the balance they have to hold between profitability and conservation of the earth's already existing resources.

Bless the children and young people of farming communities, especially those who have to move away from their homes to find work. May skills and attitudes continue to be passed on from generation to generation.

Bless those who farm in difficult and rugged places, who raise crops in unfriendly and unpredictable climates, who shepherd flocks on steep and remote mountain land or wild and lonely moors.

Bless the work of veterinary surgeons in their care of farm animals.

Bless the social life of the rural communities as it is shared in the village hall, local organisations, and the village pub.

Finally, bless the work of the church and all ministers and members of country churches and parishes. May they provide a focus of care and community identity.

Through Jesus Christ our Lord.

A confession
Father, forgive what has been done in the past when the few, in pursuit of wealth, exploited the many:
    when skills were poorly rewarded,
    when profits were shared unjustly,
    when families lived in poverty and ugly surroundings,
    when conditions of work were hard and dangerous.
As we open our lives to your forgiveness, may we constantly open our minds to ways of honouring and protecting the labour and skills of men and women.

A thanksgiving
Father, accept our thanks for the resources of industry that, from one generation to another, have helped to create the nation's wealth. We remember those whose inventiveness has improved the quality of people's lives, those whose skills have provided the artefacts of the modern world, and those industrial communities who, often through great hardship, have forged strong ties of solidarity. Teach us, Father, to take no one's work for granted.

Intercession
Lord, we pray for all industrial communities.
    For communities built around historic sources of wealth — the coal-mining towns and villages, the ship-building towns; communities that grew around steelworks; and those that relied on the railways as their chief source of employment —
        we pray, remembering especially those that have had to face changes leading to high unemployment and the fragmentation of community life.
    For communities built around new sources of wealth, the new technologies, the computer industries, the car industries, and all who contribute to the complex needs of the modern state —
        we pray, remembering especially those who have never experienced the hardships of the older communities nor known the strength of their solidarity.
Lord, let us remember that we are all members of one another.

A thanksgiving

Father, we thank you for all who are willing to accept the responsibilities of local government. We thank you for their diversity of opinions and for our freedom to choose between them in the ballot box. We thank you for those who are motivated by a true concern for the welfare of the communities within which they serve. We thank you for their unselfish commitment of time, thought and energy. We thank you for the rich tradition of public service passed from one generation to another.

Intercession

We pray for those who serve as councillors. May they be thoughtful and wise in their decisions, and open in their approach to changing conditions.

We pray for council employees. May their skills and experience be respected by elected councillors, and their dealings with the public be marked by helpfulness, courtesy and tact.

We remember the services to people for which local government is responsible. May the most vulnerable members of the community be supported and encouraged in their quest for a full and useful life.

We remember the amenities provided by local government. May well-kept parks, adequate recreation facilities, clean streets, and a humane balance between the needs of pedestrians and motorists, together contribute to a sense of civic pride and communal well-being.

Lord, may the broad strategy of local government not lose sight of details, nor a concern for policies become forgetful of people. May the quality of administration be reflected in the quality of community life, that our area may be one in which people are happy to live.

A voter's prayer

Father, may I not live as if the welfare of this community and the quality of its corporate life were none of my concern. Keep me alert to what is happening around me.

A confession
Lord, forgive those things that weaken our sense of community and
the realisation that we are responsible for one another's happiness.
Forgive the unquestioned prejudices that stand in the way of good
relationships with other people.
Forgive the indifference that leaves decision-making and social
concern to others.
Forgive the limited vision that can see issues only in terms of the
advantages to be gained by those of our own class or outlook.
Forgive the philistine spirit that inflicts ugliness on others, the
ugliness of bad planning, hostile environments, and acts of
civic and private vandalism.
Forgive, Lord, all that stunts the growth and diminishes the dignity of
the people amongst whom we live.

A thanksgiving
Lord, I thank you for this place in which I live; for the good things
that take me by surprise:
carol singers outside a supermarket, dappled sunlight in a town
square, the welcome sight of a bus on a rainy day, a candle at a
restaurant table, the sound of children playing in a park, daffodils
in Spring:
nothing much, but enough to lift a day again and make me glad that
I live here.

Intercession
Lord, increase the sense of community that binds us one to another.
Bless the work of the local church that it may:
give a sense of identity where now there is none,
provide a refuge to those who feel threatened by the anonymity
of urban living,
create a place of belonging where people know they are
welcomed, remembered by name, valued as individuals,
celebrate a faith that, in the Word, announces that we are
forgiven and accepted and, in the Sacrament, gathers us
again into the life of the Risen Christ.
For your Name's sake.

THE NATION TO WHICH WE BELONG

For the media   **Day 11**

Do not let any unwholesome talk come out of your mouths, but only what is helpful for building up others according to their needs, so that it may benefit those who listen. And do not grieve the Holy Spirit of God . . .   *(Ephesians 4.29, NIV)*

A thanksgiving
Father, thank you for the gift of word and image.
> Thank you that, in Christ, you confirmed the power of the word and sharpness of the image, for, in him, the word became flesh and, in him, we beheld your divine image.
> Thank you that, in Christ, I am called to responsibility in my use of words: my 'yes' should mean 'yes' and my 'no' should mean 'no'.
> Thank you that, in Christ, the world itself becomes a means by which your truth is made plain to us.

For Christ, in whom we see your divine glory,
we bless and praise your holy name.

A reflection
This is an age bursting with words and images. We live our lives against the background of mountains of newspapers and magazines, and the television set, flickering in a corner of the room. We can so easily become deaf to what we are hearing and blind to what we are seeing.

Intercession
Father, we pray for all who are responsible for communicating facts and opinons, through the media or word and image.
> We pray for newspaper editors, journalists, feature writers and reporters, that they may not distort the truth nor bend words into instruments of propaganda.
> We pray for television producers, presenters, script-writers and camera-men, that their words and images may be faithful to the whole picture.

Through Christ, the true and living Word.

Invocation

Lord God, lead us towards that Kingdom where every man and woman will live in the dignity of the children of God. May then we work and create as joyously as you did in the beginning. Until then, may we forge partnerships in which each uses his ability to give to each according to his need.

A confession

Lord God who, in the beginning, rejoiced in the work of creation,

forgive us when we make work a form of repression, and our places of work a field of battle;

forgive us for unimaginative, insensitive and non-consultative forms of management, that alienate workers and threaten livelihoods;

forgive us for aggressive attitudes that sour relations between workers and management, and amongst workers themselves;

forgive us for the confrontational outlook that we have inherited from the past and the mistrust that makes change difficult;

forgive us for placing our sectional interests first, even when, by so doing, we endanger the welfare of others.

Intercession

Lord God, we pray for good relationships between all levels of the work-force and management within the industries of our land.

We pray for trade union leaders and shop stewards, remembering all that they do for the welfare of their members and the improvement of work conditions:

may they lead in ways that will protect the rights of their members, increase the efficiency of their industries, and provide reliable service to the wider community.

We pray for managers, remembering the responsibility they carry for the success of their industries:

may they invite their workers to share that responsibility and devise systems that will make each person's work meaningful.

We offer our prayers through Jesus Christ our Lord.

Where study springs from vision and serves its demands it becomes an endless voyage of discovery . . .

> *(Gerald Vann, 'The Heart of Man')*

A student's prayer

Lord, may this be one of the most enjoyable times of my life.
> Give me the joy of intellectual challenge,
>> the power to concentrate,
>> the openness to assimilate new ideas
>> and the determination not to give up
>> when the going is hard.
> Give me friends with whom to share these years,
>> friends who will stimulate my own thinking,
>> friends who can be trusted,
>> friends to share the adventure of growing.
> Give me teachers who will help me to see
>> what I have never seen before,
>> and set me on a lifelong pursuit of knowledge.
> Give me a growing understanding of myself
>> and a realistic perception of my gifts,
>> that I may know how best to use my life.

Intercession

Lord Jesus, whom people called 'Rabbi' — teacher, you have set our feet on a pilgrimage to the edges of knowledge, to that perilous place, demanding nothing less than faith, where time meets eternity, and what is finite meets what is infinite.

Grant to all teachers the gift of inspiring their students, that they may have the intellectual courage to go beyond what they already know and have experienced.

Bless the work of universities, polytechnics, colleges of higher education, and vocational training schools, that they may offer excellence in their teaching, compassion and awareness in the pastoral care of their students, and an environment in which nothing is to be feared from the truth.

Give wisdom to all responsible for the funding of higher education that generations to come may have even greater opportunities than those who went before them.

*Discharge your obligations to all men; pay tax and toll, reverence
and respect, to those to whom they are due.*   *(Romans 13.7)*

A thanksgiving
Lord, we thank you for the freedom that we have inherited and for the
sacrifices of those who made them possible. We thank you that we
have the freedom to choose those who shall govern us. We thank you
that they have the freedom to ask for our support. We thank you that
the strength of our nation rests upon agreement between government
and governed, between politicians and people.

A confession
Lord, forgive us when we allow power to corrupt us,
   and save us from that absolute power which corrupts absolutely.
Forgive us when policies are put before people,
   dogma before debate,
   self-seeking before sacrifice,
   and rancour before reason.
Forgive us all that embitters and divides our common life.

Intercession
Lord, we pray for all those who follow a political calling.
   Strengthen them in the burden of responsibility that we place upon
      them.
   Guide those who shape political programmes that they may plan
      for the good of all society,
      and not set neighbour against neighbour,
      class against class,
      region against region.
   Encourage those who act as advocates for the oppressed within our
      society, and who seek to channel political power into the cause
      of justice for everyone.
   Renew the vision of those whose brightest hopes have been
      tarnished by cynicism, and whose energies have been sapped
      by frustration.
   Give wisdom to those who are faced with difficult problems, who
      must balance the necessity for compromise against the ideas in
      which they believe.

An invocation
Lord God, you have given us the law
   to restrain what is evil
   and encourage what is good.
      You gave Israel the Ten Commandments
      to be for all of us the pattern of law-making
      and the basis of civilised society.
      In Jesus you gave us the Beatitudes,
      that deeper law of the Spirit,
      by which to shape our lives
      and set our hearts on godliness.

A thanksgiving
Lord God, we give you thanks for those who have devised the laws
upon which our values and security depend:
   for governments whose laws
      protect the rights of the individual,
      make compassion an attribute of the State,
      and set limits to human folly and wickedness;
   for those who administer the law with skill and experience to
      ensure that the law will not be separated from justice;
   for the police forces who uphold the law and detect crime.
Deliver us from governments that enact bad laws,
      from lawyers who have no concern for justice,
      and from police who abuse the trust placed in them.

An intercession
Lord God, we pray
   that good people may never have cause to fear the law;
   that in places of urban and racial tension, the police may uphold
     the law in ways that will not lead them to be mistrusted by
     minority groups;
   that in the work of the courts, judges, magistrates and juries may
     administer the law fairly;
   that your Church may never remain silent in the face of injustice,
     nor isolated from the political processes through which laws are
     made.

Our society is faced with a dilemma. On the one hand, there is the terrorist who threatens the fabric of society, and on the other, the non-violent and conscientious protestor who cannot always successfully keep within the limits of the law.

A confession

Lord, forgive us when we help to create a society in which people refuse to listen to one another.

Forgive 'single-issue' dissenters whose passion for their cause distorts their perception of everything else.

Forgive those who view all dissent as subversive and will not listen to the case that others are trying ro make.

Forgive the use of violence, by dissenters who resort to indiscriminate terrorism, and by society when it suppresses the voice of dissent.

Forgive us when idealism becomes a form of tyranny and conformity an expression of intolerance.

A prayer of intercession

Lord, we pray for those who seek ways of showing their dissent.

We pray for trade union picket lines and for those who conscientiously try to cross them.

We pray for dissenters from government policies who organise protest marches.

We pray for those who keep vigil outside nuclear sites and foreign embassies.

May passions not run so high that reason has no chance of survival.

May slogans not replace dialogue.

May over-reaction not lead the forces of law into brutality.

May freedom never itself become the victim of free speech and public protest.

Through Jesus Christ our Lord.

A thanksgiving

Lord Jesus Christ, we remember with thanksgiving your ministry among us. You made blind people see, deaf people hear, lame people walk. You gave hope to all who are disabled. Lord, we thank you for the continuing miracle of that hope. We thank you for all that transforms the life of people with disabilities: for the courage that overcomes handicap, for the medical technology that reduces the limitations imposed by disability, for the rich contribution made by disabled people to the life of society.

A confession

Lord, we pray that you will forgive our ineptitude in relating to people with disability.

> Forgive us the embarrassment that makes us awkward and unnatural in responding to disability.

> Forgive us our failure to think imaginatively into what it means to be blind, or deaf, or paralysed, or disfigured.

> Forgive us when our prejudices and our failure to take account of the needs of disabled people, impose upon them a greater disadvantage than the disability itself.

> Forgive us when we treat deaf people as if they were daft, and blind people as if they were helpless, and people in wheelchairs as if they were an inconvenience.

A prayer of intercession

Lord, we pray that people with disabilities may be enabled increasingly to take their place, on equal terms, in the active life of our society.

> Bless the work of architects as they design buildings giving full access to people with disability.

> Bless those who advocate the cause of disabled people, spokesmen who are themselves disabled, their relatives, those who are responsible for the services that assist them, and those legislators who argue for the provision of greater facilities.

> Bless all people with disability, that from them we may learn something about ourselves.

When Jesus was at table . . . many bad characters — tax-gatherers
and others — were seated with him and his disciples; for there were
many who followed him.   *(Mark 2.15)*

A reflection
Who are our 'bad characters'? Perhaps our problem is not so much
the bad, as the foolish, the weak, the accident-prone, the deeply
unhappy, the inadequate. Our off-hand language conceals their
plight: junkies, winos, wierdos. We hide ourselves, because their
intractable problems are an offence to our well-ordered, rational
world.

> Lord Jesus Christ, may I not turn my face from the plight of those
> who have fallen through all the safety nets of home, school and
> society:
>> the drug addict with bruised arms and sunken face and wild
>> dreams,
>> the winos, a fragile fellowship passing a bottle from mouth to
>> mouth,
>> the homeless drifter asleep in a hostel bed or huddled under a
>> cardboard box in a sheltered doorway.
> Like the 'tax-gatherers and others' they do not fit easily into
> society; yet they fit into your compassion.

Intercession
Pray for drug addicts, for their families, for those who work in
rehabilitation.
Pray for alcoholics and for their families, remembering not only
those who have taken to the streets, but those whose illness is
concealed behind the walls of their homes and hidden from their
colleagues at work.
Pray for the homeless who have no roots, who have lost themselves
in the anonymity of the city.
Pray for those who work amongst people in desperate need, small
action groups in local churches, the Simon Trust, Alcoholics
Anonymous, the Salvation Army, the state-run hostels and all
other agencies of compassion.
Lord, be with them.

A thanksgiving

Lord, we give you thanks for the gifts of those whose creative talents enrich our lives.

We thank you for fictional authors from whose imaginations there leap characters, plots, and stories which cast a spell around us and lure us into their intriguing, tragic, unpredictable, urbane and funny worlds.

We thank you for composers whose music has been our companion, remembered for the exhilarating moments in which it lifted us, for the tunes we sang on unspectacular days, and the rhythms we drummed with our fingertips.

We thank you for poets and their power to give words to those depths in our experience which we believed to be beyond all words.

We thank you for performers whose skills at the keyboard, string, wind, brass and percussion make music for our delight.

Lord, in the beginning, when you had created all things, the morning stars sang for joy. We thank you for the echoing songs that still encircle the earth, rising in gladness with the sun and singing in the lyrical stars of the night.

A celebration

Blessed be the Lord for the worship of heaven and earth,
    breaking like countless waves on unseen shore.
Blessed be the Lord for the words of worship,
        for prayers that utter all that is in our heart,
        for preaching that is fire and light,
        for liturgies that unite us with the church triumphant.
Blessed be the Lord for the songs of worship,
        for the great hymns of the faith,
        for the music of a pilgrim people,
        for chaste Gregorian chants
        and intense charismatic choruses.
Blessed be the Lord who accepts the offering of our praise
    and rejoices to be with us in our worship.
            From the rising of the sun to its setting
            The Lord's Name is to be praised.

A thanksgiving
Lord, we give you thanks for the land of our birth:
  for its language and all who have taught us to use it well;
  for its history, its architecture, its books;
  for its varied beauty, its mountains, fertile fields, rivers and seas;
  for its industrial wealth and the traditional skills of its peoples;
  for the diversity of its regions.

A confession
Lord, there is a patriotism that is blind, and a pride of race and blood
that is blasphemy. From such patriotism, good Lord, deliver us.
Forgive us the fear of foreigners, outsiders, strangers
  that makes us defensive, intolerant and arrogant.
Forgive us national slogans that summon us to racial isolation
  and away from our responsibilities
  within the family of mankind.
Forgive us that devotion to our own cause
  which muffles our conscience
  and makes us capable of withholding justice
  and inflicting cruelty upon others.
Forgive us that selfishness
  which robs us of magnanimity.

A prayer for our place in the world
Lord, may citizenship of our own land prepare us for citizenship
within the universal community of mankind. May the wealth of our
own heritage make us more appreciative of the heritage of others.
May the ways in which we learn to live with our own diversity, and
discover unity in the midst of our own differences, prepare us for the
task of peace-making and reconciliation in the wider world. May we
not hanker after an imperialist past, nor yearn for a totalitarian future,
but bear with gladness the responsibilities of freedom, and look with
confidence to the gathering of the nations. May we live in the
knowledge that all nationalities are provisional, until that day comes
when the kingdoms of this earth become the kingdoms of our God.

For the United Nations Organisation Day 21

A thanksgiving
Lord God, we give you thanks for the birth of the United Nations Organisation out of the conflicts of the Second World War.
Thank you for the vision of the early days,
> for the hope that was nurtured in the dark post-war years,
> for the occasional and successful intervention of the Organisation in areas of conflict,
> for the work of service agencies in areas of education and health,
> for the Organisation's stubborn commitment to international co-operation, even when it has been weakened by cynicism from the inside and criticism from the outside.

A confession
Lord God, forgive everything that stands in the way of international understanding.
> Forgive our fears of one another that lead us to use our vast resources of power for potential destruction rather than dealing with the areas of human need.
> Forgive our nationalist and racialist posturings that make it difficult for us to work comfortably together.
> Forgive our contempt for imperfect institutions in an imperfect world.

Lord, deliver us from fear,
> deliver us from arrogance,
> deliver us from the search for perfect solutions.

Intercession
Pray for the Secretary General and all permanent staff,
> for diplomatic representatives,
> for all the Organisation's service agencies.

*He will judge between many peoples and will settle disputes for strong
nations far and wide. They will beat their swords into ploughshares
and their spears into pruning hooks.*   *(Micah 4.3, NIV)*

A confession

Lord, forgive us that we spend more of our skills on 'swords and
spears' than on 'ploughs and pruning hooks': the terrible 'swords and
spears' of our own generation, weapons of mass destruction, capable
of inflicting incalculable suffering.

Forgive the lack of will that prevents us from ridding the world of
such weapons.

Forgive the fears we foster, nourish and make strong on a diet
of mistrust and mis-representation.

Forgive us for wasting time when time is short.

Intercession

Pray for experts and negotiators who, through the long months and
years, sit at the conference table seeking ways of scaling down the
world's arsenals.

Pray that their skills may impel them towards the goal of
disarmament with a greater sense of urgency.

Pray for national governments, that they may take as many risks in
the quest for peace as they now take in the interests of national
security.

Pray that patience may not be lost nor any set-back to negotiations
lessen the determination to reduce the stock-piles of weapons.

Pray for a spirit of *detente* between divided nations, that disarmament
negotiations may be conducted in an environment of growing trust.

Pray that, one day, a generation will be born that no longer has
cause to fear the human capacity for destruction.

May the dreams of the prophets come true and the prayers of the
faithful through all generations be answered, as your will is done on
earth as it is in heaven, through Jesus Christ our Lord. Amen.

> *How blest are the peacemakers;*
> *God shall call them his sons.*   *(Matthew 5.9)*

So he came and proclaimed the good news: peace to you who were far off, and peace to those who were near by; for through him we both alike have access to the Father in the one Spirit.

(Ephesians 2.17-18)

A thanksgiving

Lord, thank you for all men and women who have the gift of making peace.

They break down the well-preserved walls of division.

They build again the bridges that have fallen into disrepair.

They discover a common language by which enemies may again speak to one another.

They point out the alternatives to hostility, hatred, war, aggression and battle.

They are the faithful ambassadors of reconciliation.

Lord, they are your sons and daughters in whom the Good News is heard more clearly.

Intercession

Lord, we pray that the peacemakers may stand in the great divide between East and West, and bring together those whose enmity threatens the entire world.

We pray that they may reconcile North and South so that both may sit together at the table of plenty and none go away hungry.

We pray for their presence in the Middle East, in South Africa, in Ulster, that today's forgiveness may bind up yesterday's wounds and prove tomorrow's hope.

We pray for their advocacy of the Gospel where human unbelief sets man in enmity to God, that Christ's blood-bought peace may make us all the friends and servants of God.

A prayer for ourselves

Lord, create in me a love for peace: not peace that is the absence of struggle, nor peace that is blind to injustice, but peace that makes whole what now is broken.

Invocation

God our Father, the only barriers to the earth's riches are those that we have built. Poverty remains in the world, not because you will it, but because we perpetuate it. Hunger sits at the doors of our plenty because of human indifference. May we, with Mary, rejoice in him who comes to fill the hungry with good things and send the rich empty away. May no one be hungry where your love and lordship are acknowledged.

'When I was hungry, you gave me food; when thirsty, you gave me drink; when I was a stranger you took me into your home, when naked you clothed me; when I was ill you came to my help, when in prison you visited me . . . anything you did for one of my brothers here, however humble, you did for me.'   *(Matthew 25.35-36,40)*

A thanksgiving

God our Father, accept our thanks for those who go swiftly to the aid of people in need.

Thank you for aid teams who work in famine-stricken areas.

Thank you for those who draw on modern technology and the labour-intensive skills of indigenous peoples to husband the resources of the earth in more effective ways.

Thank you for the poor who give back to us the humanity of which our wealth can rob us.

Thank you that the Christian faith calls us, not to competition but to compassion, not to build a fortune but to bring in a Kingdom.

Intercession

Father, we pray for the work of people and organisations who provide aid in areas of human need:

for Christian Aid, Oxfam, Save the Children, Tear Fund;

for Mother Teresa in Calcutta

and for others similarly engaged in the hand-to-hand conflict with human need.

We pray for governments, that the needs of the universal family of mankind may be an important factor in assessing the national budget.

*Countless thousands of our fellow human beings today live under
tyrannical governments. On left and right of the political spectrum,
cruelty has become an instrument of government.*

A confession

Lord, we acknowledge the sins of those of our fellow beings who are
    the agents of tyranny.

Lord, we acknowledge the sins of unjust courts that administer unjust
    laws and prop up unjust societies.

Lord, we acknowledge the sins of jailers, torturers and executioners,
    whose cruelty is ever with us.

Lord, we acknowledge man's terrible inhumanity to man.

Lord, judge the sins of human hands,
                the dark cruelties of human hearts,
                the wickedness of human minds,

and, in your terrible mercy, bring the guilty to repentance.

Intercession

Lord, we pray for the victims of oppressors.

We pray for populations who are denied the freedom of political
    debate and intellectual enquiry.

We pray for men and women in the prisons and camps of oppressive
    regimes:
        for those in solitary confinement,
        for those who are tortured,
        for those who have been imprisoned
            for many years.

We pray for the families of those who suffer,
        for the children of prisoners of conscience,
        for wives and husbands whose years of marriage are spent in
        waiting and in praying for the day when the prison doors will be
        opened.

We pray for all who daily remind us of their plight and whose
    vigilance knows no rest.

For places where terror is born
Father, we pray for those places in the world
whose history and political circumstances
have made them the breeding grounds of terrorism.
We pray for children who are raised
to become another generation of terrorists;
for children who are taught the ugly lessons of history
in order to keep alive the injustices,
indignities and atrocities of the past;
children who are taught the ways of violence
and drawn into armed conflict.

'As for the man who is a cause of stumbling to one of these little ones
who have faith, it would be better for him to be thrown into the sea
with a millstone round his neck.'   *(Mark 9.42)*

For those who suffer at the hands of terrorists
Father, we pray for those who, suddenly and brutally, find
themselves in the hands of terrorists.
   We pray for people who are kidnapped and have to live through
   the ordeal of capture, uncertainty, abuse and the constant threat of
   death itself.
      We pray for those who have been wounded and maimed by
      terrorist activities, whose bodies are a daily reminder of the
      outrage that was committed aginst them.
   We pray for innocent people who are in the wrong place at the
   wrong time and who become the victims of other people's
   disputes.
      We pray for those who have been bereaved by terrorist violence
      and who live with the bitter memory of lives cut down before
      their time.

For an end to the way of the terrorist
Father, we pray for effective deterrents and safeguards against
terrorist activity. We ask that the root causes of the terrorism may be
dealt with effectively. Grant that we may together learn better ways of
resolving our conflicts.

A thanksgiving

Lord God, you are the creator of all things and you continually sustain
the life of the universe and all that is within it.

We thank you that you have called us to share in the work of caring
for what you have made.

You have made us your partners and have led us into the mysterious
secrets of your universe.

You have revealed to us the resources hidden in your creation and,
through the skills of scientists, physicists and engineers, you have
taught us how to use them effectively.

You have placed us in a position of great responsibility within the
animal kingdom.

Lord God, accept our thanks for this green and fertile planet and for
the place you have given us within it.

A confession

Forgive us, Lord, for the damage we have done to the earth.

Forgive us that the rivers and seas have been polluted by the waste
of our civilisation.

Forgive us that the air has been turned foul by burning fuel and
radio-active emissions.

Forgive us that flowers, fauna and wild creatures have become
extinct through our relentless invasion of their natural habitat.

Forgive us that we have often valued profit more than the quality
of the environment in which people have to live.

Intercession

Creator Lord, we pray for those who struggle to preserve our world
and who remind us of our responsibilities within it.

Bless those who fight to protect endangered species.

Bless those who monitor the threat to natural resources
posed by our scientific advance and industrial expansion.

Bless those theologians who continue to remind us
of the relevance of our belief in the Incarnate Christ
to our stewardship of material things.

A thanksgiving
Father, we thank you for the struggle of men and women, in every age, who have fought for a more equal society. We thank you for those who withstood political tyranny, even at the cost of their lives. We thank you for those who have led minority and racially disadvantaged groups from the twilight to a place in the sun. We thank you for those who have embodied, in national and international laws and statements, safeguards protecting the rights of all men and women. We thank you for a growing awareness of human rights and an unwillingness to see them denied.

A confession
Forgive us, Father, when human rights are withheld from anyone.
Forgive us when people have no say in who will govern them.
Forgive us when people are denied the right to food and adequate shelter.
Forgive us when people are denied the right to work.
Forgive us when people are denied access to justice and to an impartial legal system.

Intercession
Pray for the rights of minorities to be free of persecution, harassment and discrimination.
Pray for the right of women, within the family, within society, and within the church, freely to choose the role they wish to play, and exercise the gifts that they have been given.
Pray for the right of the sick to adequate medical attention with compassionate and skilful care.
Pray for the right of people to live their lives in the place of their choosing.

Father, side by side with all the rights you have granted as our human legacy, you have set the duties that we owe to you and to one another. May we honour those human duties and thereby ensure the honouring and upholding of human rights. Through Jesus Christ our Lord.

Jesus said, 'Full authority in heaven and on earth has been committed to me. Go forth therefore and make all nations my disciples; baptise men everywhere in the name of the Father and the Son and the Holy Spirit, and teach them to observe all that I have commanded you. And be assured, I am with you always, to the end of time.'

(Matthew 28.18-20)

Reflection

Lord, that you love *everyone* is more than my imagination can grasp. The earth teems with people; we lose sight of one another's individuality; in a single day we recognise only a fraction of the faces we see. We live in a world of strangers. Yet no one is a stranger to you. You have not lost count of the human race. There is no heart that you do not know as well as my heart; no one lives in a far country beyond the reach of your love. So help me to see that your love is beyond my imagination and greater than I can ever understand.

A thanksgiving

Lord, thank you for the mission of the church that has not ceased since the days of the apostles.

Thank you for those who brought the gospel to our own land and led our forefathers into the Christian way.

Thank you for those who have been in the spearhead of Christian mission and have been prepared to go wherever you called them.

Thank you for all that we have to tell others:

> your presence amongst us in Jesus Christ,
>
> his death for us on the cross,
>
> the liberating experience of the resurrection.

Intercession

Lord, we pray for the spread of the gospel.

> Bless those who preach, teach, heal, build, reconcile, bring hope, that their message may be the means of salvation to those who hear;
>
> and grant that your Church may grow and increase in the knowledge of your divine love.

With deep roots and firm foundations, may you be strong to grasp, with all God's people, what is the breadth and length and height and depth of the love of Christ, and to know it, though it is beyond knowledge.   *(Ephesians 3.18)*

A confession
Lord Jesus Christ, head of the Church, we acknowledge the sins of your people.
> We have built walls that have shut out the world and separated us from one another.
> We have been slothful in working through the beliefs in which we are divided,
> too ready to retreat to the tired vocabularies of yesterday,
> too eager to hide behind the familiar,
> too mistrustful of the good intentions of others.
> We have wearied in the long haul of ecumenism, settled for what we have, and lost our appetite for what courage and faith could still give us.

Intercession
Lord Jesus Christ, we pray for the divided churches of Christendom.
> We pray for our brothers and sisters of the Roman communion, thanking you for the wealth of their spirituality and its increasing enrichment of our own prayers.
> > We pray for our brothers and sisters in the Eastern churches, thanking you for their witness to the power of the resurrection to renew the life of all creation.
> We pray for our Protestant brothers and sisters, thanking you for their devotion to the holy scriptures.
> > We pray for our Pentecostal brothers and sisters, thanking you for their joyous witness to the presence and gifts of the Holy Spirit.
> We pray for the radical house churches who have turned their backs on us and ask that we may not be lost to one another.

Lord, the more we grow to understand one another, the more grievous become our divisions and the more offensive the barriers to Christ's holy table. Unite us first in love and then in Word and Sacrament.

An Act of Praise

Lord, the whole earth awaits your coming.

> From all our earthly Jerusalems, we look for the coming of the
> New Jerusalem, the holy city of God.

> Above the sound of our snarling quarrels and our shouted insults,
> we hear the new song that you have set in the mouths of your
> people.

For you come to us,

> not with a rod to break us,
>
> nor bleakly resembling our military might.

> You come, showing us in ways that we have hardly begun to
> grasp, how love prevails.

> You come, in the resurrection, breaking the power of that before
> which we are powerless.

> You come,
>
> the Lord of life and death,
>
> the God of time and eternity.

And already all creation awaits you and begins to greet you.

> The desert longs for the life you will give to it.

> The mountains bear their silent witness to your faithfulness.

> The seas lift their waves to greet you and in their profound depths
> speak of unfathomable love.

> And men and women,
>
> wounded by sin and made whole by forgiveness,
>
> finding courage in their fears
>
> and peace in their adversities,
>
> made in your image and bearing your Son's likeness,
>
> wait, most longingly, for the coming of your Kingdom.

Lord, until the day dawns,

> keep us firm in our faith;
>
> make us faithful in our duties
>
> and diligent in using the gifts you have given to us.

> May joy not desert us,
>
> nor hope ever cease to be our companion;
>
> and, above all things, may love grow and increase amongst us so
> that, at your coming, we will not be strangers to each other.

THE CHRISTIAN YEAR

Advent Sunday

Only you,
Advent God,
can turn winter into spring
by a new birth of hope amongst us.
Only you
can turn darkness into light
by transforming flesh and blood
into infant splendour.
Only you
can remove the weight of guilt
which crushes our humanity
by offering your forgiveness
and unlocking a new day.

Then come to us.
    Enter our winter,
            our darkness,
            our guilt,
    and with December daring
    live once more in woman, man and child.
    Bring to birth
    in every tired heart
    a spark of eternal energy
    which will blaze a trail of peace on earth
            and glory in the highest.
    Bring to birth
    a change of heart and will
    within those whose power is great
            yet whose vision is blurred.
    Enable hope to grow
    in city waste and rural desert
    and in all the places
    where magnificat is never sung.

Fill with confidence every patient Christian person
who in this season searches for your presence
and proclaims your surprises to a sleeping world.

Second Sunday in Advent (Bible Sunday)

God,
your voice is not distant.
    It addresses us
    where we eat, work,
    travel and play.
Your voice is not threatening.
    It takes away
    our fear and guilt
    touching the deepest parts
    of our lives.
Your voice is not confusing.
    It speaks plainly
    about justice and hope,
    pleading consistently for peace,
    taking up the cause of silent sufferers
    who weep for a redeemer.

Speak your word through our conversation.
Lead new people to discover your mind
    through the passion of your prophets today.
May the acts of contemporary apostles
    form compelling evidence of your Spirit's power.

As we cherish the Scriptures
and read of your surprises,
    let your word penetrate our prejudices,
    uncovering our false motives and hypocrisy.
As we hear your urgent call
to Abraham, Moses and Elijah,
    remind us that these are people like us,
    wondering, doubting, travelling, risking.
As we reap encouragement
from psalm, song, proverb and parable,
    may our lives leap for joy in thankful worship.
As we explore the meaning of your coming in Jesus,
    heighten our expectation of your power
    to fill the world with good news
    and summon all created life
    to belong to your Kingdom.

Third Sunday in Advent

Lord,
I remember how Bethlehem was a shambles:
     full of activity yet unprepared
     for its cosmic guest.
And that's how it is with my life, Lord.
I've a Christmas card list which reads
     like a Roman census.
I've guests to plan for and presents to pack.

Help me to stop
and begin a different kind of preparation.
Help me to take stock of my priorities,
     my relationships, my hopes,
     so that I am in the right frame of mind
     to embrace this season
     with its promise of peace,
        its announcement of joy,
        and its opportunity to make a new beginning.

Fourth Sunday in Advent

Lord,
as you dispelled
the fears of a maiden mother
by whispering the promise of your presence,
so banish
the world's misconceptions
about you and your ways.

Come to each of us.
Roll back the clouds of doubt and pessimism.
Fill our individual lives with servant love
and direct the nations to humble awareness;
     for you are God,
     rich in mercy,
     strong in righteousness,
     ready to make your home with us
     now and for ever.

Christmas Eve

Living God,
let candles be lit and our eyes be bright
to reflect our joy at your coming.

Remind us
how this Christmas night
the waters of creation
broke with hope
and a mother's pain
brought forth a human child
swaddled in divinity.

Take us back in time
to when tears of joy were shed
and shepherds' strength surrounded
this precious babe
whose kingdom still fills the universe with hope
and whose birth is every person's new beginning.

Christmas Day

Jesus,
new-born child of all time,
we greet your birth
with wide-eyed delight.
You are precious beyond words
for our world needs your presence more than ever.

Let the angels' promise of your good news
offering joy and peace to all the world
be heard by those who lead and guide.
Let kings bow down
and all creation greet this holy moment
as we seek to grasp its magnitude.

For you are God's gift
silently delivered
to every human heart.

Epiphany

Shine brightly,
star of God,
and guide our wandering world
to where a Prince of Peace is born.

Where children wish upon a star
or wise men scan the universe in hope
let your bright beams
surround their dreams
and guide their hesitating feet
to where a miracle is born.

Enable each of us
to make a New Year's journey
leaving behind the prejudices and fears
of yester-year,
embracing a fresh openness
by which we welcome all world pilgrims
whose journeys end in worship and humility.

Be a sign today
of mercy and of love
like a rainbow in spring
or the bright summer sun,
and show us how our lives
can include the forgotten and forlorn
                the grieving and the hurt.

And we will offer
to our God
now seen and touched in straw-filled bed
the best gifts in the world:
our joy, our grief, our life.

Ash Wednesday

Lord,
on this day
we remember how so often
garlands turn to grief,
hosannas to jeers,
palm leaves to ashes.

This Lent
we pray that you will conquer death within us:
    save us from the death of our minds
        through our dogmatism and emotionalism;
    save us from the death of our personality
        through our laziness and indifference;
    save us from the death of our humour
        through self-importance and unnecessary worry;
    save us from the death of our nation
        through blindness to poverty and fear;
    save us from the death of our world
        through our empire-building and narrow nationalism;
    save us from the death of our spirit
        through superficiality and secularism;
    save us from the death of our churches
        through hypocrisy and blindness.
Rather give us life:
your full and fine life
which deepens and grows
through outloving the world's hatred
and outgiving the world's greed.

Then may our discipleship
be a pilgrimage of joy
and not a journey of duty,
brim-full of encouragement for others
bursting with commitment to Jesus
who carries the burdens of his world
and covers the cost with suffering love.

First Sunday in Lent

Jesus,
you were not spared
the harsh decisions
and you did not run away
from the difficult choices we all have to make.

May this strengthen us
when we are tempted to take short cuts,
putting off the pain,
avoiding the struggle.

Make us suspicious of those who offer us
power and glory
in order to fulfil their wishes.
Make us wary of those who hold out
popularity and acclaim
for promoting their dreams and goals.
Give us courage to avoid
the quick and easy solution
to deep-seated problems.

Come close, we pray,
to those who are in positions of power
in politics, industry and the civil service,
especially where corruption
can easily affect decision-making
and situations can be turned to personal advantage.

Rid your Church
of all that promotes status and prestige,
and make your people
servants of humanity
loving only you
worshipping none other
but your name now and for ever.

Second Sunday in Lent

Lord,
we are so like your first disciples,
eager yet blind,
excited yet fearful.
Sometimes we glimpse the secrets of your kingdom
but often our eyes are clouded by misunderstanding.
Sometimes we hear the truth you proclaim
but often our ears are not tuned to your voice.

Like James and John
    we grasp selfishly for the prizes;
like Philip and Thomas
    we are pessimistic and doubtful;
like Peter
    we are strong one moment then weak the next.

Have patience, Lord.
Forgive us
our short-sightedness
and muddled thinking.

As we follow you
amid the dilemmas of our time
give us new courage and strength
so that our lives
may proclaim your truth
and enable others
to see, hear and understand.

And when we let you down,
disowning your name
and handing over
fresh crosses for you to carry,
please forgive us
and raise us from our grief
to serve you in renewed joy and love.

Third Sunday in Lent

Jesus,
what sort of king are you?

The world's ways are so different,
Our rulers talk of success and progress,
                    security and status,
                    prestige and power.
Yet our eyes are drawn to you,
                    a Saviour in sandals,
                    a king without a palace,
                    a leader with bowl and towel.

Remind us of the fragile nature of power.
Now that Rome has fallen
and Britain doesn't rule the waves
teach us a new humility
so that we can understand again
what is most important to our peace,
our joy and our future.

Help all who lead the nations
to learn the lessons of history
so that a new international community can emerge
which is not ashamed of dependence
            not afraid to take risks for peace.

Come close, we pray,
to those whose path as nations
leads them at this moment through suffering,
humiliation and oppression.
Be present
with your Church where for your sake it loses its life
and experiences weakness and pain.
Watch over
those individual Christians
who face the darkness of persecution.
This we pray
for your own name's sake.

Fourth Sunday in Lent

Jesus,
more than a prophet,
more than a law-giver,
recognised by God
if not by those whom you came to serve,
we rejoice that you have fulfilled
all that was best of the past
and that you now become for us
the focal point of history,
the goal of our journeyings.

We recall the precious moment when in shining splendour
your name was raised above all names
and your painful work was displayed
as the Father's purpose for the world he loved.

let this be the focus of our worship
now and for ever
as in praise
we marvel how the way of the cross
could be the way of our redemption.

By your mighty work of salvation
transfigure the face of the world
so that it shines with love,
radiates with justice
and glows with peace.

And if we feel secure and safe
on our mountain-tops
or in our churches
bring to our ears
the cries of an epileptic world
whose pain can only be assuaged
by your kind of power,
healing and compassion.

Fifth Sunday in Lent (Passion Sunday)

God,
it's always tempting to believe
that when we become followers of Jesus
we are spared the torment and tears of the world;
it's tempting, too, to imagine
that your Son Jesus
has done all the cross-carrying that is necessary.

Keep on reminding us
that discipleship is about taking up new crosses,
that we are not protected from the cruelty of human beings
or the unanswerable circumstances of nature.

Then
weeping with those who weep
and laughing with those who rejoice
show us how we can enter into life in the world
completely and whole-heartedly
trusting you as Lord of it all.

Be near to those whose faith is tested to the limit
by personal suffering and sudden grief,
offering through us to them
the genuine comfort of those who know
that you can gather up human pain
into your enormous heart
and make it the means of declaring your grace and love.

As Jesus our Lord
was raised up in crucifixion,
so lift up in our lives
those unusual qualities of meekness and unselfishness
which the world derides as weak.
Bring glory
to lives lived in faithfulness to the truth,
to nations who seek justice and peace,
and to your church where it follows
your way of suffering love.

Palm Sunday

Let children wave flags
and stones shout 'Hosanna'
to greet you, Jesus,
as today we celebrate
your entry into Jerusalem.

Show us once more
the sort of king you are:
humble, peace-loving, righteous.

With you
we pray over Jerusalem
and every city
which through the centuries
has never known peace and freedom.

How long, O Lord,
before we learn the ways of peace?

How long before we abandon
the way of terror and the bomb?

How long before children
can walk the streets in safety
and laughter can be heard
instead of weeping?

Inspire us today
and every day
to struggle and serve
with energy, enthusiasm and commitment
until the people of violence
hear the cries of the peace-makers
and understand that the God you came to proclaim
is Lord of the nations and cities
and judge of all the earth.

Maundy Thursday

Bend your back,
royal Saviour,
and wash the dust from human feet.
In clearest lines
draw for every generation
the picture of how you want the world to be:
a community of footwashers,
a people who never tire of serving
> of stooping
> of washing
> of laying aside the garments
> of power and glory.

Tonight we remember you
in bread and wine
aware that when your body is broken
and your blood is spilled
in all corners of the earth
it is a sign reminding
the power-hungry and bloodthirsty
that no cause can prosper
unless it is rooted in your servant heart
and no empire can be glorious
unless it is based upon your servant will.

Then
every time
we share the communion
our thanksgiving abounds
as you join us with all your friends
who promise to love the world
as you have done,
and as you whisper
your shalom
to every soul,
confirming your Easter presence.

Good Friday

Father of Jesus
broken and dying, tormented and lonely,
we have no words
which can express the shame of this day.
Your only son, uniquely loved,
hangs bleeding because of us,
crying for our forgiveness.

We deserve nothing, Lord,
Night covers our world,
              our hearts, our lives.

Yet in his agony
he draws our gaze
and the full scope of your eternal love
seems to flow over us
like a mighty river
drowning our sorrows and guilt.

What a mystery, Lord,
belongs to this day.
What secrets it holds for every century,
every nation and every soul.
Let this tree become the tree of life
for every weeping child
and may those arms reach out
to hold in your embrace
a cruel world
which needs your mercy in its night.
Let Jesus, crucified and raised,
bind up the wounds
of every suffering community
and lift the cloud of guilt
which covers the earth.

Only then can we be surprised by your joy
and greet your resurrection day.

Easter Day

Living, glorious God,
the universe rejoices
and every voice is shouting Hallelujah,
for you have triumphed today.

Every obstacle has been rolled away;
light has penetrated the dark tomb;
fearful joy has replaced the heaviness of grief.

Our lips break into singing;
our unbelieving eyes meet those of our Risen Lord,
and we are raised to life.

If you,
in devastating love,
can create an Easter dawn
from Friday's deathly night,
then can there be a stronger sign
that we are loved eternally?

Nothing now
can separate us from your motherly arms;
nothing now
can come between us and your embrace;
nothing now
can deprive you of your power to build the earth
on the foundations of forgiveness and peace
until your kingdom come.

So we add our voices
to the praises of all creation
and,
reborn every day,
we will proclaim your victory
in lives of hope
and words of joy
and deeds of courageous service;
all because of Jesus
our loving, Risen Lord.

Ascension Day

Mighty God,
your work on earth in Jesus Christ
fills us with wonder and thankfulness.

Jesus,
born in humility,
who died in disgrace,
you have raised to the heights
so that his name can be known
in all the universe
as Lord of lords and King of kings.

We praise you
that his way of sacrificial love
by which he did not cling to any thought
of status or reward
has been shown to be the only true way
to life and joy and peace.

We praise you
that his way becomes the way of those
whom he now calls to share the work of your kingdom,
and we ask that your Church
in all the world
may never lose sight
of the essentials of this ministry.

Let any power we seek
come from you;
let any glory we seek
proclaim your victory;
let any name we announce
draw attention only
to Jesus Christ,
our ascended Lord.

Pentecost

Loving God,
we rejoice
that you have not left us as orphans
without support, comfort or direction.
Now that Jesus' earthly work is complete
your resources are not diminished
and we praise you today for your Holy Spirit,
sign of your active presence in the world.

Open our lives to embrace your power
so that we are living parts of Christ's body.
Make us witnesses to your Gospel
so that by the fruit in our lives
others are brought closer to the kingdom.

Then may the babel of nations
be transformed into one single language of peace
and your Spirit speak a new word
to the nations.

Fill your Church
with the best gifts
of faith, hope and love
so that her unity in the Spirit
may come before rivalry and prejudice.

Lead us into your truth
as we seek the mind of Christ
through the wisdom of your Spirit,
and may our worship
be enriched by the many gifts
you provide for your people.

Move ahead of us, stirring, enlivening,
and carry us forward to share your surprises
for you are the flame of energy,
                the dove of peace,
                and the breath of life
for all your people.

Trinity Sunday

No words, eternal God,
can describe your character and worth.
No language can encompass
the mystery of your presence and power.

We struggle for phrases,
pictures and words,
but all in vain.
You are too large, too full of wonder
for the mouth or pen.

You are God, eternally One,
Mother and Father of all creation,
loving and forgiving beyond our imagining.
You draw from us our praise
in all times and places.

Yet in Jesus Christ
you become a Word made flesh,
a person to be touched and seen.
In human weakness you shed your power
and tread the path to life and death.
And we are shamed and torn
to see you carrying our grief.
Crucified you draw from us
a new and deeper worship
for worthy is the Lamb
to receive all our allegiance.
In him we see your face.
In him we are raised to life
with Easter splendour.

But you have more to show us, living God.
By your Holy Spirit you lead us into new discoveries.
In a miracle of love
you make us your children,
and call us to suffer and serve
in all the world
making visible your grace in Jesus Christ.

OCCASIONAL PRAYERS

'For everything there is a season . . .'   *(Ecclesiastes 3.1)*

a time to be born . . .

Loving God,
you are the beginning and end of all creation.
I rejoice in the gift of life
seen in every new-born child.
I am reminded how dependent I am
upon your goodness and love.
The dawn of each new day
becomes an opportunity
for me to be thankful to you
for those who have nurtured that life within me.

. . . and a time to die

Dying, rising God,
you are eternal and loving
always seeking to take away my fears.
In Jesus you have shared my every experience.
Please be near each person who is dying
especially where through guilt or ignorance
they have not come to know you as a God of mercy.
Give to the very old and the terminally ill
your serenity and peace
and bless those who wait, nurse and pray.

a time to plant . . .

Lord,
whether I am sowing seeds of hope
in dry and depressed lives
or sowing seeds of possibility
in an arid neighbourhood,
or simply enjoying my garden or greenhouse,
it's all part of your miracle of growth.
Make me content to sow and plant
and ready to wait for the harvest
with patience and care.

. . . and a time to pluck up what is planted

Bring to fruition, Creator God,
the work of your kingdom.
Make us part of that joyful harvest
in which your loving purpose is completed.
Help us to realise
how important the smallest words and deeds are
    in the context of eternity.
At harvest time when we remember your goodness
    make us grateful also
        for all we have received from the labour of others
        who have sown the seeds of faith, hope and love
        in our lives.

a time to kill . . .

God,
forgive us
for the personal hatred and jealousy
which destroys our relationships
      stifles neighbourliness
        and leads to open acts of violence.
Help us to recognise the situations
where words and deeds out of place
can cause immense damage,
and so guide our ways
that we do not increase the death
so rampant in the world.

. . . and a time to heal

Use me, loving God,
to bind up the wounds
of all whom I discover on my journey.
Show me how I can work out my priorities
so that I have time not only for emergencies
but also for that ongoing, long-term serving
which comes
from constant availability
and dependable care.

a time to break down . . .

Lord,
where communities are fragmented
and families split up
    in a hectic, mobile world,
come close
so that even in situations of change and uncertainty
your spirit of togetherness
can work with power;
and when my own life is dislocated and disoriented
show me your consistent presence and power.

. . . and a time to build up

Lord,
thank you for the people of encouragement
who always make me feel bigger, stronger, livelier,
and for those who build up others
when their confidence has been destroyed.

May my outlook transform others also
as I try to be like Jesus was to his friends —
truthful, honest, open, eager to step with them
into your future.

a time to weep . . .

Jesus,
you wept over Lazarus your friend
and over Jerusalem your city,
and we too are deeply saddened
by personal tragedy and international disaster.

Show us how we can weep with those who weep
so that we come alongside others in their darkness
rather than judging them for their faults,
as you have done with us and for us
in the Father's name.

. . . and a time to laugh

Father,
thank you for those
whose wit and humour
have lifted me from the gloom
teaching me to laugh at my world,
        myself, and my fellow human beings.
Thank you too
for the way laughter has healed the world
helping to remove the silly prejudices
which are so damaging to our life together.

a time to mourn . . .

Lord,
where tears fall
through tragedy or heartbreak
enter the silence
and hold me tight
lest in bitterness I blame you
or those close to me
when I should be trusting you
with those I love
and groping my way towards gratitude
for the time I have been privileged to share with them.

. . . and a time to dance

Living God,
let my faith be rooted in delight,
celebrating your presence
in joy, brightness and festivity.
Let me proclaim you as a God
who is Lord of the dance
lightening my steps,
joining me to others
and bringing a smile to my mixed-up world.

a time to cast away stones . . .

Lord,
when it is time to say 'goodbye'
to friends, family or places we love
give us courage
to move on to new experiences
to make new associations
and to allow our children the freedom
to create their own journeys in life.

Where families face division and separation
so that individuals can rediscover their own identity
please be near to sustain and guide.

. . . and a time to gather stones together

Thank you, Father,
for all homecomings
     all rediscoveries of friendship
which make us realise
how important the past is
and how much we need a sense of continuity
in our relationships.
You are a thread through all our comings and goings.
Never let us ignore you
or the part others have played in our lives.

a time to embrace . . .

Loving God,
you have embraced your world in Jesus Christ
wrapping it round with new hope and security.
Let my life do this for others;
let the Church encircle those in dire need of love;
let the deepest moments of love we experience
be signs of how the world is meant to live
in Jesus' name.

. . . and a time to refrain from embracing

Lord,
when I need to be on my own
to think
to wonder
to decide
give me that space and room
to be alone.
Gently provide for me
the resources to cope with what I have to face
and lead me back to those I love
renewed in body, mind and spirit.

a time to seek . . .

Jesus,
Shepherd extraordinary,
I remember how your energy was spent
in looking for those rejected by society
        and by religious institutions.
Make me aware of those
        left out in conversation
        left behind in the race for wealth
        ignored in social gatherings
        forgotten by government and Church.
Then give me the courage not to stand still
but to include them into your family.

. . . and a time to lose

Lord God,
sometimes I need to be reminded
that I cannot do everything myself.
Show me how I can give to others
the things I am tempted to do myself,
so that in Christian service
they are encouraged to use their skills.
Show me, too, when it is time to let go of vital tasks
and pass on the mantle to others you have called.

a time to keep . . .

Loving God,
we are surrounded by so many possesssions
many of which we feel we need
but lots of things are not as necessary
as we imagine.
Help us to keep what is essential
to our health and our service to others.
Help us also to keep what is best from the past
living eagerly in the present
and not afraid to look forward rather than back.

. . . and a time to cast away

Lord,
let there always be a time in my life
for letting go
of the things I depend on too much:
my wealth, my self-importance,
my unnecessary luxuries,
the many things I take for granted.
Then may I realise how much I owe you.
Make giving a way of life for me
not so that I can be applauded or congratulated
but so that I can remind myself daily
that this is the way you relate to me.

a time to rend . . .

Lord,
when I have to say things
which hurt others
or when I have to make a decision
which leaves someone unhappy
be near to encourage a spirit of understanding.
And when in our local and national life
groups have to separate because of conviction or conscience
let your spirit of tolerance bring about
an acceptance of others' points of view.

. . . and a time to sew

Lord,
I pray today
for all who spend their precious time
bringing together those who are divided and alienated:
people who mend industrial disputes,
family frictions, racial unrest.
Help me never to ignore opportunities
in my own experience
to bring lives together
and create new understandings between the estranged.

a time to keep silence . . .

Lord,
in a demanding, noisy world
give me moments
when all I can hear
is the sound of a bird
or the rustle of the leaves.
Thank you for time to stop
     time to wait
     time to pray
time to be with someone to whom
I don't need to say anything.

. . . and a time to speak

Loving God,
forgive me
for often lacking courage
to say what needs saying
when I hear statements which are prejudiced,
  misleading and hurtful to others.
Make me more determined to risk unpopularity
so that those who have no voice
can find encouragement
through what I dare to say.

a time to love . . .

God,
you are the source of love
and you join us together in the miracle
of friendship, marriage and family life.
Let faithfulness, freshness and unselfishness
fill the deep relationships we cherish
and be a sign to the nations
that this is the way you love the world
in Jesus Christ our Lord.

. . . and a time to hate

God,
even with those who are closest and dearest
there are moments of anger and hurt.
Please have patience with us
when we destroy what is beautiful
through our failure to listen
and through our obsession with ourselves.

a time for war . . .

God of nations
past and present,
you weep over the violence and pride in your world.
We too cry out for those forgotten people
whose homes, land and daily life
have been devastated by the folly of distant nations.
Lord, have mercy.

. . . and a time for peace

Bless the peacemakers, Lord:
the quiet, strong people
who strive night and day to help us understand
what our enemies are saying.
May we do all we can
to make our time a time of peace.